Tale
of the
Three

A Rescue Story

By Sharon Elizabeth Colwell
Illustrated by Kathryn Marie Brewer
Edited by Leah Elizabeth Brewer

A true story

WestBow Press books may be ordered through booksellers or by contacting:

WestBow Press
A Division of Thomas Nelson & Zondervan
1663 Liberty Drive
Bloomington, IN 47403
www.westbowpress.com
844-714-3454

Because of the dynamic nature of the Internet, any web addresses or links contained in this book may have changed since publication and may no longer be valid. The views expressed in this work are solely those of the author and do not necessarily reflect the views of the publisher, and the publisher hereby disclaims any responsibility for them.

Cover and Interior Art Credit: Kathryn Marie Brewer

ISBN: 979-8-3850-1526-9 (sc)
ISBN: 979-8-3850-1528-3 (hc)
ISBN: 979-8-3850-1527-6 (e)

Library of Congress Control Number: 2023924258

Print information available on the last page.

WestBow Press rev. date: 02/22/2024

These are times of non-communication between parents and their children, between children and children, between friends and friends, and between teachers and students.

Technology has replaced skills such as talking with each other, teaching our children virtues, and, most importantly, listening to each other.

Virtues, or doing what is right and avoiding what is wrong, are not being taught to our children. Common virtues such as charity, patience, gratitude, and kindness are sadly lacking in our youngsters.

Taking responsibility for one's actions and being responsible for God's creation are also inadequate in our youth today.

This book is a true story that demonstrates many of these concerns. The questions for discussion at the end of the book will hopefully stimulate meaningful communication regarding these concerns and will also lead the readers to practical solutions of the problems presented.

PROLOGUE

Grandma almost always had a dog. Before she was born, the family acquired a dog named Husky, who was a two year old brown, white, and black long-haired pooch. Grandma did not know how the family acquired Husky. All she knew was that she always loved him and he was her dog for as long as she remembered.

Grandma had Husky for twelve years. She did everything with him. They played outside in all kinds of games. She took him for walks, strolls down the alleys, and even climbed trees with him. Husky was not allowed inside, but if no one was home, he somehow found his way into Grandma's bedroom. Ever vigilant for the sound of the family car, Grandma would push Husky out of the window and act as if all was normal.

Grandma and Husky

Sadly, Husky was not put in a fenced area and was free to roam. When he was twelve years old, he was hit by a car and died soon after. Some people like to refer to a lost pet as "crossing the Rainbow Bridge". That is what happened to Husky.

Grandma missed Husky so very much, but she would not be without a dog for very long. One day, a little brown and white puppy wandered into Grandma's yard. It was "love at first sight". Grandma named him Terri and was so happy. And, lo and behold, Grandma's dad said she could keep the pup!

However, several days later, a man knocked on the door and asked to see the pup. He had noticed the pup in their yard, and he said that his new puppy was missing. Oh, no! Well, Grandma started to bawl and bawl. But, the kind man said Grandma could keep the pup! Grandma was so, so happy. She had a dog to play with, explore with, and watch grow up.

Those years were filled with loving Terri. Grandma had Terri for six years. The summer after high school graduation, Grandma drove her grandparents on a road trip to California to visit relatives. When she got back after two weeks, she could tell that Terri was not feeling well. Unfortunately, after a few days, he "crossed over the Rainbow Bridge". Grandma was again so sad.

But life got busy, especially now that Grandma had begun college. She wanted very much to be a veterinarian but found chemistry and physics to be very difficult. So, she decided to become a biology teacher. Grandma also got engaged and was married following her college graduation.

And then, another puppy! This little guy was a cute, tan and white terrier who Grandma named Duff. He became her new "puppy love". After several years, Grandma had another "precious love" and that was her first child, a little girl! After several moves, the family settled in a small town and welcomed another precious daughter.

During this time, sadly, Grandma's sweet dog Duff got out of the fenced yard and was struck by a car. Another dog "over the Rainbow Bridge".

Through the following years, three more children were born and many more dogs spent special times with Grandma and Papa. They were Max, Willy, Pete, Brownie, West, and the rescues Kort, Libby, and Tinker. After those pups, Grandma and Papa bought Charlie and Jenny. There was also one cat named Noah, another rescue, who joined Grandma and Papa's home as well.

Each and every one of those pets could be a separate book in itself. However, this book is focused on the last three dogs, Solavina, Duke, and Tiffi, as well as Noah, the cat.

Chapter 1:

GRANDMA LOVES GARAGE SALES

Grandma has always loved to go to garage sales. This began when she and Husky would travel down the nearby alleys and look for the "treasures" that residents would set out by their trash cans. Empty soda bottles would be great finds because Grandma could cash them in for five cents a piece at the grocery store. Grandma would then use the money to buy soda, gum, or candy! Grandma also found many other items that people had thrown away. She once found an old typewriter and actually used it all four years of college to type her assignments.

As Grandma got older, she would drive her car to attend garage sales and estate sales. She spent many Saturday mornings attending these sales and finding her "treasures".

Many years later, on one particular Saturday morning, Grandma was going to a garage sale and turned onto a dirt road. Just then, she came upon a small bunch of puppies that seemed to be about two months old. As she was watching them play, she suddenly noticed that one of them, a little brown one, had an empty peanut butter jar stuck on its nose! No telling how long the jar had been stuck on the pup's nose, but Grandma knew she had to do something. She grabbed the pup and then noticed a larger, black and white female watching her. That was the mama dog!

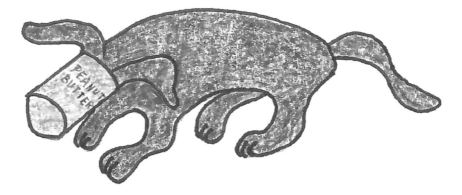

Tiffi with her head stuck in a peanut butter jar!

About that time, an older couple came out of their small home and began to watch all the happenings. Grandma went to them and explained that the puppy could not get out of her predicament without their help.

The couple turned out to be Frances and James. They told Grandma that the week before, someone abandoned the pups and their mama on their street. They fed the dog family a few food

3

scraps, but they were not able to feed them enough to keep them healthy. They were upset that the dog family had been dumped and left to make it on their own.

Grandma asked James for a pair of pliers to try to remove the jar from the brown pup's nose, but James did not have any tools. Grandma thought about Papa. He had lots of tools and was a very kind man. So, Grandma put the pup in her truck and headed to her house!

Grandma heading home with Tiffi

At Grandma's house, Papa was all ears at hearing the pup's story. He was successful in removing the plastic jar from the pup's nose. Now, one must know that Grandma and Papa had their last dog, Charlie, pass over the Rainbow Bridge just one month before. Grandma and Papa thought, "hmm, maybe the new pup is just right for us!"

So, Grandma went back to James and Frances's house to tell them that they had agreed to keep the brown female pup, now named Tiffi. Grandma had noticed that James seemed especially fond of the mama dog, whom Frances had named Solavina. So, Grandma had a proposal for James and Frances. Grandma said that she and Papa would find homes for the remaining four pups if the couple would keep Solavina. Grandma would also see that Solavina would have an operation so that she would not have any more puppies. This would simplify life for James, Frances, and especially Solavina. They did agree to this, although a bit reluctantly.

One last question Grandma was wanting to ask was, what did the name Solavina mean? She felt that it was a unique name and had never heard it before. Frances said that it came from the Spanish word "solo" meaning alone, and the verb "venir", which means "to come". Frances explained that in Mexico, a term for a stray dog was "Solavino" for a male stray, or "Solavina" for a female stray. The name means "to come alone" as did Solavina, except she brought five pups with her!

Solavina

Chapter 2:

FINDING HOMES

Grandma made some calls and had an appointment made for Solavina to have her operation. In the meantime, Grandma got a large crate and went to pick up the four pups. Now, the pups really did not like this idea. There was a culvert with a large drain pipe in front of James and Frances's house. All four pups ran to hide in the drain pipe, but Grandma lured them out with some puppy food, that is, all but the last pup! That little one crouched as far back in the drain pipe as it could. Grandma had to crouch and bend down in order to reach her arm way into the opening. Poor Grandma, she lost her balance and her head flopped down into the culvert! Grandma was still holding onto the shrieking last pup but now could not get her head and upper body up from the trench.

Grandma stuck in the culvert

And now, oh no, Solavina heard her last little pup crying as loud as it could! Solavina decided she had to rescue her pup from Grandma. Solavina did not bite Grandma but nipped at her shoes and her legs. All this time, Grandma was desperately trying to hold onto the pup and also get her head up. What a sight this must have been! Finally, Grandma was able to get up and, with pup in tow, she put the last little pup in the crate.

Grandma's next move was to find homes for the four pups. She called several shelters but they were all full. So, Grandma being Grandma, made a big sign and took the pups to the main street of her town and set up a "Puppies for Sale" spot.

Grandma had been advised to put a "For Sale" sign rather than a "For Free" sign. The idea is that people may make more of a commitment if they have to purchase a pup rather than just take one for free. Grandma was not going to charge much; she only wanted thoughtful decisions to be made.

Grandma and her sign

After a couple of days, Grandma had found homes for two pups, but she still had two left. Finally, a sweet lady took pup number three. Now, Grandma had only one more pup to rehome. It was then that she had an "aha!" moment. Grandma reasoned that two pups would be as easy to raise as one pup, and the pups would also have companionship with each other. She talked to Papa about the idea, and he agreed! So now Tiffi had a brother, a black and white male they named Duke. The puppies were so happy to be reunited in their new home with Grandma and Papa.

Then came the next predicament! Grandma went to get Solavina at Frances and James's house for her operation but Frances was not happy. She told Grandma that she and James changed their mind and could no longer afford to keep Solavina.

So, Grandma put Solavina in her crate to take her to the appointment. Later that day, Grandma picked up Solavina and took her to Grandma and Papa's house, where she was reunited with Tiffi and Duke. What else could she do? Papa again was so sweet and accepted this arrangement for the time being. Grandma told Papa that she would try to find a home for Solavina and she did try but, well, you know!

Chapter 3:

LIFE WITH THE PACK

Grandma and Papa settled in with their new pack. "Puppies being puppies" found Duke and Tiffi wanting to chew on everything! Grandma bought stuffed animals (at garage sales, of course) for them to chew on. She also found an abandoned, old fashioned straight chair, which she put on the back deck. The pups really enjoyed eating it up! All three also had tug toys and hard chew toys shaped like bones. They also had a few "puppy accidents" on the carpet, but Grandma cleaned up the messes without complaint. Solavina was recuperating nicely from her operation and made herself at home. And how sweet and gentle all three dogs were, going from lap to lap to snuggle up with Grandma and Papa.

If the weather was nice, they spent much of the day outside in the fenced yard. As it was winter, all three of the dogs slept in the garage at night. Grandma made sure they had lots of blankets and, if it was going to be really cold, she would put out an electric heater for them.

As time went on, Papa decided that he wanted to be the one to feed the dogs. He scooped out the correct portions of dog food and fed each one in their own special bowl. He made sure that there was always fresh water for them, both outside and inside. Since the pups ate very fast, Solavina had her food bowl in the kitchen, and Duke and Tiffi were fed in the garage. They usually scattered their food all over the garage floor!

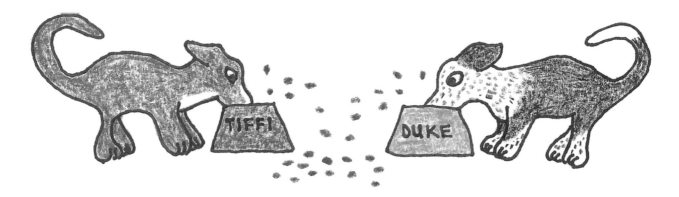

Duke and Tiffi eating

Chapter 4:

Noah

All was going well, but then came the encounter with Noah, Grandma and Papa's cat. Now, Noah had been living with Grandma and Papa for nine years. He had (of course) also been a rescue.

Noah was discovered by neighbors of Grandma and Papa when he was about six months old. The neighbors were trying to move into their rent house, but this little kitten kept trying to get through their front door. Grandma had gone over to greet the new neighbors and see if she could help. When she asked them what she could do, they asked Grandma if she could take the kitten away from their house so they could do their moving. Grandma assured them that she could find a home for this little, pitiful, crying kitten.

This kitty looked like he had been out on his own for a long time. He was thin, so thin, and had a full case of mange, leaving him with little fur. He had teary eyes and fleas galore. Well, an emergency trip to the veterinarian and lots of loving care turned this pitiful kitten into a beautiful, long haired cat who became Noah. And, of course, his new home was with Grandma and Papa!

Noah, a sick little kitten

Grandma and Papa did not even consider that the new dog family would not get along with the cat. All of the previous dogs had either tolerated Noah or even played with him. But this was not to be the case with Solavina. The first time she saw Noah, thankfully, was through the glass door. She became very excited and aggressive with her barking at Noah. Grandma and Papa knew right then that they would have to keep them away from each other. Most of the time, Noah stayed in the bedroom with the door closed shut. But one day, Solavina squeezed through the door and went into the bedroom. She attacked Noah and a big fight was on!

Luckily, Grandma and Papa were able to separate them without any harm to either one. Noah, of course, was very upset, and Grandma and Papa were even more determined not to let an encounter like that happen again.

Grandma and Papa put their heads together and added more precautions to keep those two apart. They decided to put up signs around the living room to remind them to keep Solavina and Noah apart.

Signs

Chapter 5:

THE DIGGERS

Now it was time for another episode. Grandma and Papa had a good sized backyard fenced all around. They assumed the pack would have a great yard to run in and play. But one morning, Grandma went into the backyard and noticed that the moles had dug their underground tunnels and dirt mounds.

Now, a mole is a small, rat-like critter that lives underground. When Solavina smelled the scent of the moles and saw that lovely, loose soil of the mounds, she got to digging! She dug out the moles' openings in the mounds, and dug and dug. Pretty soon her two pups, Tiffi and Duke, joined in the fun.

Moles in the backyard

After a few days of trying to shovel the soil back into the holes and trenches, Grandma hoped the problem was solved. But, oh no, now the pack decided to dig along the fence line, the whole fence line! Then, Grandma knew she had to go into full action. There was a construction site near her house, and Grandma noticed that the builder was burning pieces of scrap wood. So, Grandma being Grandma, stopped and asked the builder if she could have some of the scrap wood. After she explained her predicament, he told her to take all she wanted! Grandma was so happy and went home to get Papa's pick-up truck and returned to load up the planks. One could say that the fence line was made of boards both vertically and horizontally!

Grandma was hoping that the digging would stop, or at least slow down, and there would be no more big issues. But, sadly, that was not to be. There was a much more serious problem ahead.

Chapter 6:

THE BIG FIGHT

The morning began quiet enough. Grandma did some chores while Papa watched the television news. About mid-morning, the three dogs were in the living room as it was cold outside. Noah was in the bedroom behind closed doors. Grandma was in the kitchen and noticed that Papa had gone into the bedroom where Noah was sleeping on the bed. All of a sudden, Grandma heard Papa say, "NO!", and she saw Solavina pushing her way past Papa into the bedroom. Solavina had seen Noah!

Well, as soon as Papa started shouting at Solavina, her two pups also rushed into the bedroom and "The Big Fight" began! Noah ran under the bed as Solavina was making her way toward him. Grandma rushed into the bedroom where Papa, Solavina, and the two pups were all trying to get to Noah. All of a sudden, Noah rushed by everyone and ran into the bathroom, which adjoined the bedroom. Noah ran to the bathroom vanity in the corner and was hissing, scratching, biting, and shrieking at all three dogs.

Grandma and Papa tried to catch one dog but then another one would get to Noah. Over and over Grandma and Papa had control of one dog, only to be trying to contain another one from getting to Noah. It was quite a terrible scene! Grandma finally caught Solavina by her back legs and, after a great struggle, was able to get her out of the bathroom, then the bedroom, and finally out the back door. Papa was holding Duke and Tiffi by their legs and collars as best he could.

The Big Fight!

During the interval of getting Solavina out of action, Noah managed to get himself behind the washing machine, which was in the bathroom, thus protecting himself from the pups. Now Grandma and Papa were able to get Duke and Tiffi out the back door.

Finally the fight was over! However, Grandma noticed that Papa had been seriously scratched on his arms by the dogs' claws. Poor Papa, both his arms were bleeding and, needless to say, both he and Grandma were totally exhausted. The cat/dog fight lasted about ten minutes, but it seemed like forever to Grandma and Papa. Grandma was able to clean Papa's arms a little and noticed that he had one really bad claw mark that would need medical attention. Grandma checked on Noah and saw that he was safely behind the washing machine and appeared to be okay.

Papa with his cuts

Then, Grandma took Papa to the nearby emergency care center where Papa's wounds were treated. He had seven stitches in the bad cut and the doctor cleaned and wrapped the numerous abrasions on both of his arms. Oh yes, Papa also had to have a tetanus shot and antibiotic pills to take home!

When Grandma and Papa got back home, Grandma settled Papa into his favorite chair, and then she went to find Noah. Noah was still behind the washing machine, and Grandma was able to lift him up so that she could examine his body for damage. He showed no signs of punctures or scratches but did seem to have a hurt leg. He definitely was upset and scared and just wanted to be left alone. Grandma prepared his favorite spot, set out fresh food and water, and left him so he could rest.

All in all, Grandma, Papa, and Noah would be alright, although now some new decisions would have to be made. That was not going to be easy. So, what do you think Grandma and Papa should do?

Discussion Questions

It is not easy to find suitable answers to Grandma and Papa's problems with the dogs. Hopefully you have settled on some solutions. The following offers chapter by chapter questions for discussion.

Chapter 1

    A. Why do you think people abandon animals?

    B. What other choices do people have rather than abandon their pets?

    C. In what way were Grandma and Papa problem solvers?

    D. Do you think Grandma and Papa showed virtues? Why or why not?

Chapter 2

    A. The author wrote that when Grandma decided to take the two remaining pups and Solavina to her home, "What else could she do?". What other choices did she have?

    B. Do you think Grandma and Papa worked well together as a couple? Why or why not?

Chapter 3

    A. Why do you think Grandma did not complain when the pups had "accidents" on the carpet?

    B. Was it necessary to have a fenced-in yard for the new dog family? Why or why not?

Chapter 4

    A. Why do you think Noah was so special to Grandma and Papa?

    B. What could be done about Solavina's aggressive behavior toward Noah?

    C. What do you think the saying, "Old Habits Die Hard" means?

Chapter 5

    A. What qualities in a person are important and necessary in problem solving?

Chapter 6

    A. What are the different problems that Grandma and Papa need to consider about Solavina, Duke, and Tiffi?

    B. What does the saying, "The solution can be a double edged sword" mean?

    C. Virtues include love, joy, peace, patience, and kindness. Do you recognize any of these virtues in this story and why?

Printed in the United States
by Baker & Taylor Publisher Services